The impression Edinburgh has made upon us is very great; it is quite beautiful, totally unlike anything else I have seen.

Queen Victoria, 1842

Visitors – even royal ones – tend to give Edinburgh rave reviews. Built around a centuries-old hill fort, Edinburgh has seen many battles, but has been at peace since 1746 and today impresses visitors most with its dignified grandeur and proud beauty.

The city is a mix of startling contrasts: a sumptuous palace and a dour, indomitable fortress; a warren of haphazard back streets and an architectural blueprint for the best in Georgian town planning. Edinburgh has a strong military tradition which it combines with its world-famous festival of artistic creativity.

This photographic guide celebrates the best of Scotland's capital city.

EDINBURGH CASTLE

Edinburgh Castle sits upon a rocky core of an extinct volcano which rises up to 133 metres (436 feet) above sea level. There has been a fortress here for around 1,400 years.

Queen Margaret, the English wife of King Malcolm III, spurred Edinburgh's development in the 11th century. The crude stronghold was converted into a royal castle and Queen Margaret died here in 1093. When her youngest son, David, became king, he dedicated St Margaret's Chapel to his mother's memory. It is Edinburgh's oldest surviving building.

For centuries, Edinburgh Castle has been a symbolic and strategic prize in the battles between Scotland and England. It was razed to the ground in 1314 but later that century began to evolve into the form we see today.

The castle approach features an esplanade, a parade ground built in 1753, where every year the Military Tattoo is held during Edinburgh's summer Festival. The ornamental castle gatehouse was built in 1887. Surmounted by the Royal Arms of Scotland, it is flanked by statues of Scottish heroes Robert the Bruce and William Wallace.

Crowning Castle Rock are the main castle buildings: a palace occupies three sides of a courtyard known as Crown Square and the Scottish National War Memorial the fourth. The **palace** was built in the 15th century. It contains the tiny bedchamber where Mary Queen of Scots gave birth to James VI of Scotland in 1566. He was later crowned King James I of England, uniting the two countries.

The palace also houses the Honours of Scotland – the crown, sceptre and sword of state – in the **Crown Room**. The crown of Scottish gold was remodelled for King James V, although it is thought to incorporate the circlet worn by the rebellious Robert the Bruce at his hasty inauguration at Scone Abbey in 1306.

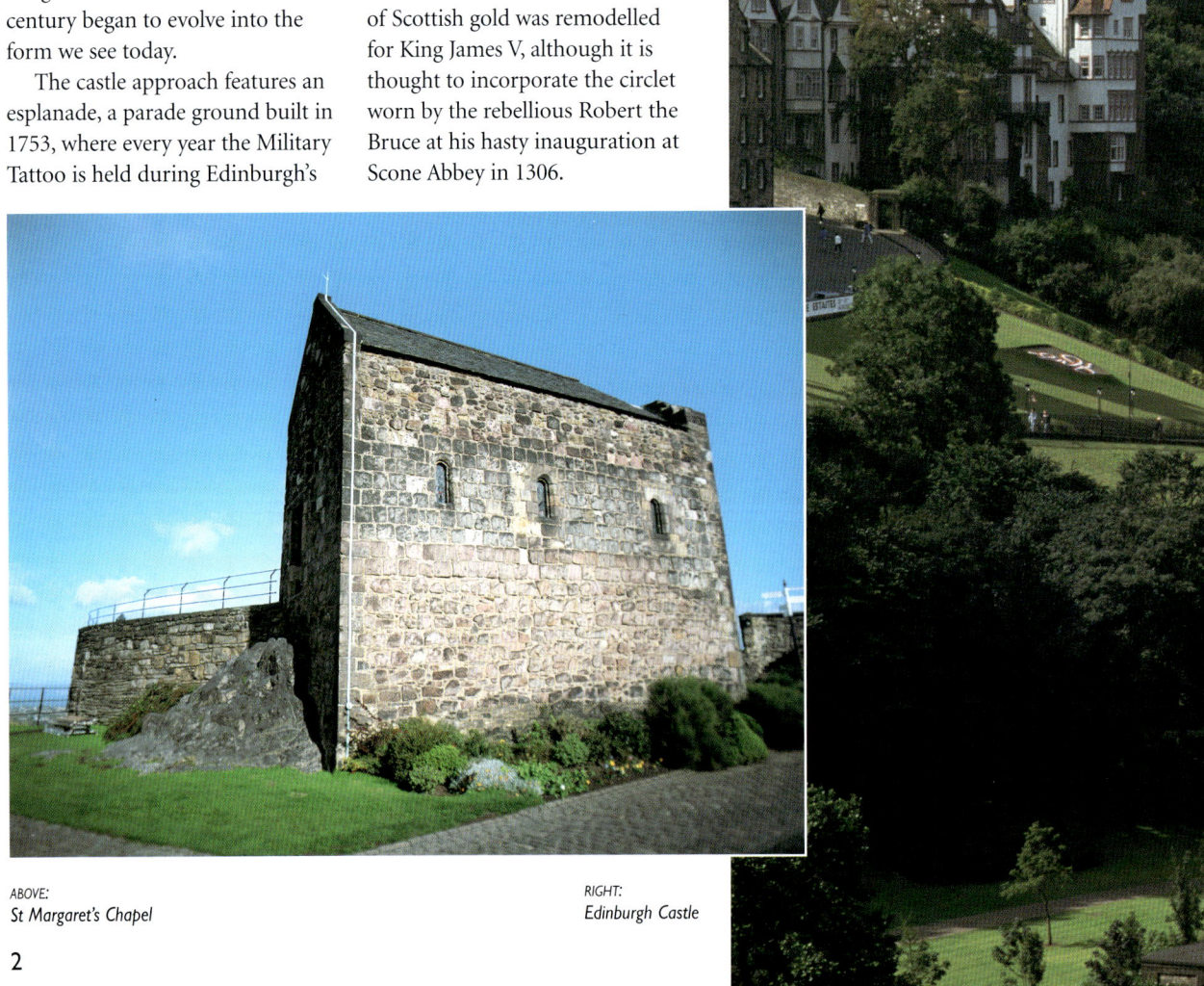

ABOVE:
St Margaret's Chapel

RIGHT:
Edinburgh Castle

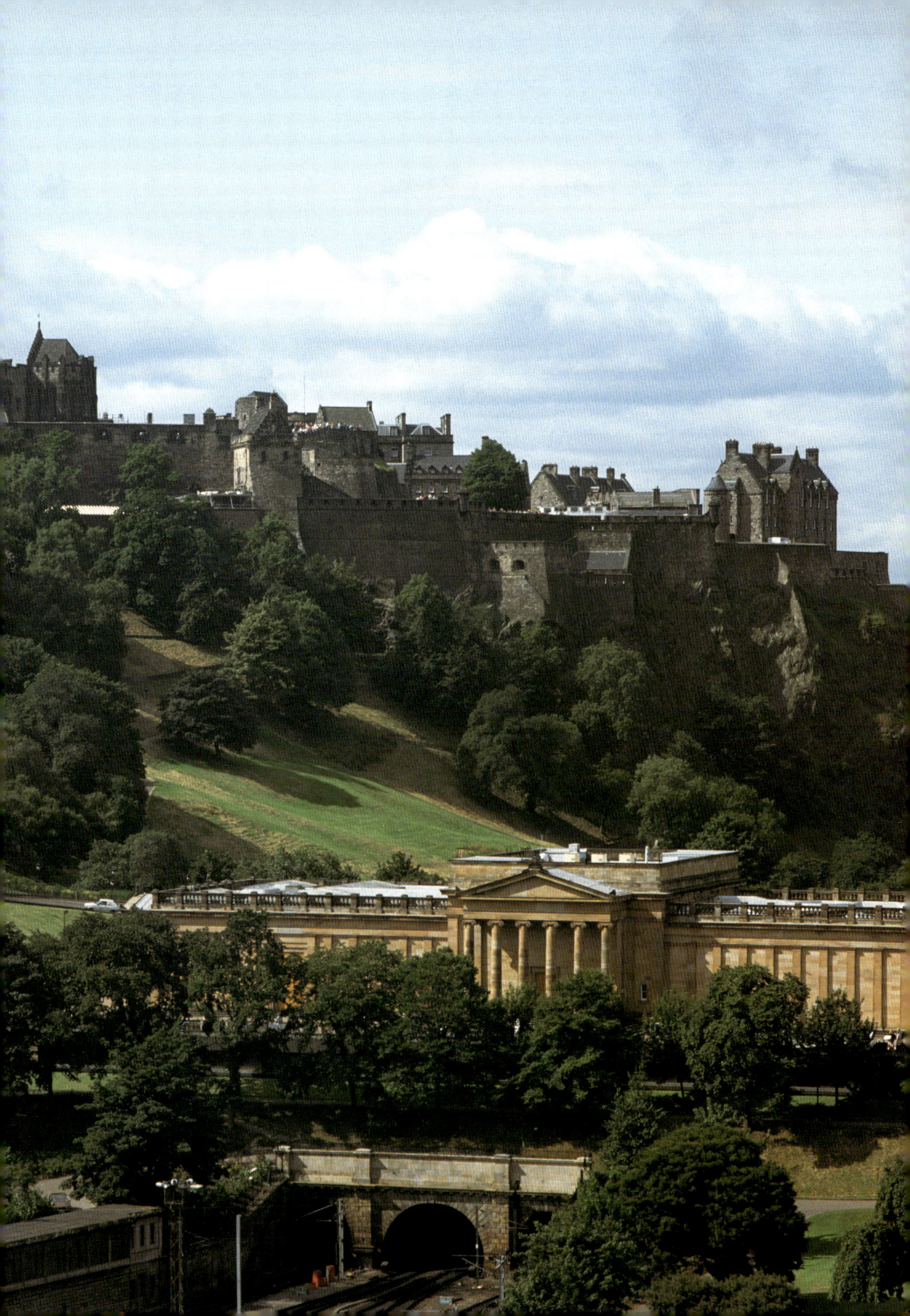

LEFT:
Fireworks launched from Edinburgh Castle during the Festival

RIGHT:
The room where Mary Queen of Scots gave birth to her son James

BELOW:
The cannons that fire the one o'clock gun are next to the old cart house, now a restaurant and shop

In 1996 history was made when the Stone of Destiny was returned to Scotland. According to legend, this stone was brought to Scotland from the Holy Land, and was the rock upon which Jacob had laid his head. It was housed in Scone Abbey and for centuries kings of Scotland sat upon it for their inauguration.

However, in 1296 Edward I defeated the Scottish forces and, to strengthen his grip on Scotland, took the Stone of Destiny to Westminster Abbey. On 30 November – St Andrew's Day – 1996, the Stone was returned to Scotland to take its place alongside the Honours of Scotland.

Part of the palace is now the **National War Museum of Scotland** with displays of military weapons and uniforms. The Scottish National War Memorial was built after the First World War and honours the nation's war dead in that and later conflicts.

The **Great Hall** dates from the early 16th century and was the meeting place of Scottish Parliaments until 1640. It was built by King James IV as a banqueting hall and as a setting for ceremonial occasions. Restored in the 19th century, the hall features displays of arms and armour and a notable hammer-beam roof. Below the Great Hall are the vaults, now known as the French prisons. They were used in the 18th and 19th centuries to incarcerate French prisoners of war.

From the Castle's battlements salutes are still fired by cannon to mark special occasions. Every day (except Sundays) a gun is fired at one o'clock as a time check. The castle's most famous cannon is massive **Mons Meg**, which was given to James II in 1457 and weighs 5 tonnes. Reputed to be able to fire its huge cannon balls 1.5 miles, it is now housed in the French prison (or vaults) beneath the Great Hall.

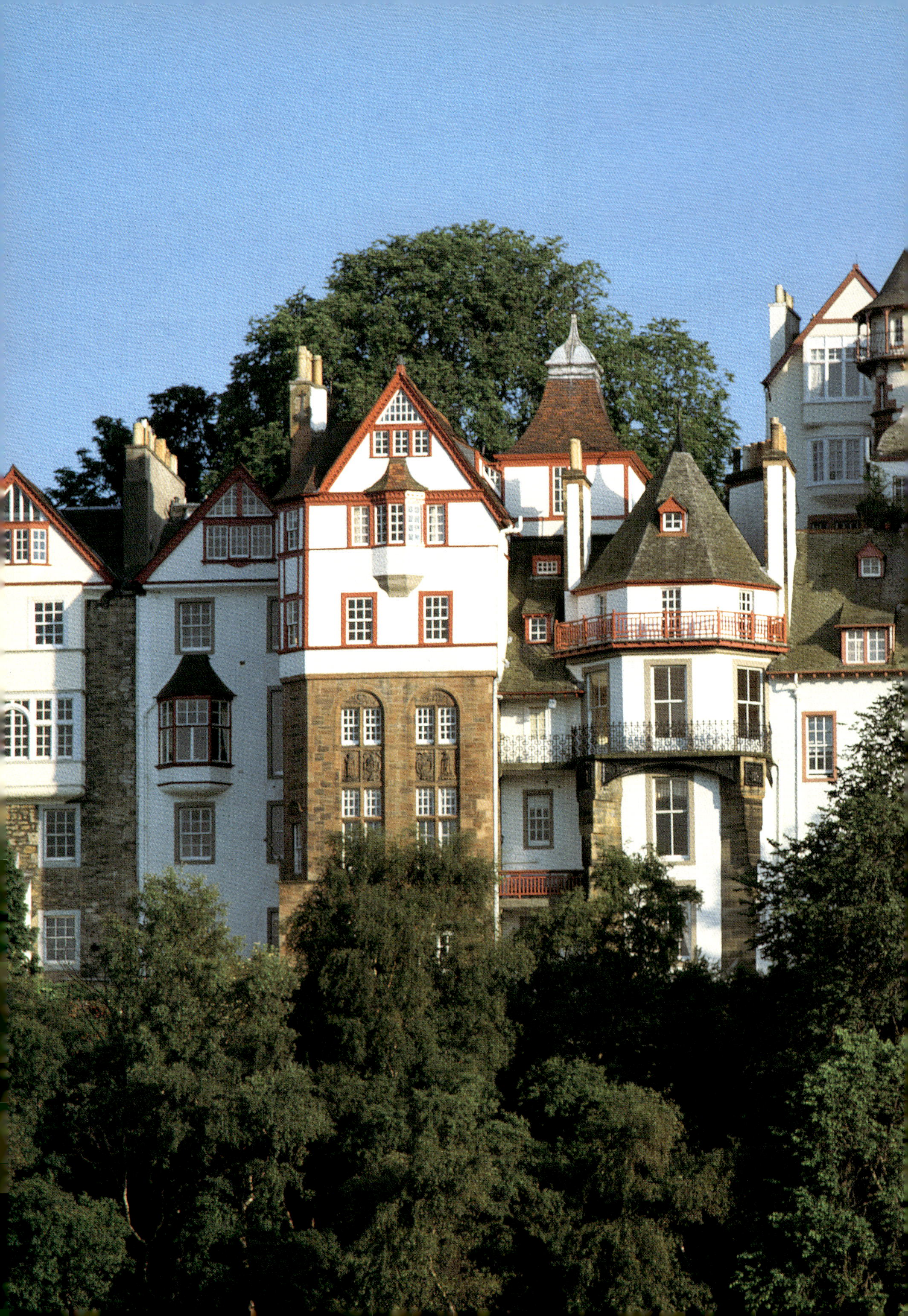

THE ROYAL MILE

Edinburgh's development spread outward from a huddle of buildings in the shelter of the castle and along a rocky ridge leading to the Palace of Holyrood. The route is called the **Royal Mile** and the area around is known as the Old Town.

The Old Town is characterised by its tall houses set in wynds (narrow streets or lanes) and closes (blind alleys). **Castle Hill** is the oldest street in Edinburgh. Conflicting stories surround the name of Cannonball House, built in the 17th century. One explanation is that a ball lodged in the wall during the siege of the castle in 1745. Another is that the ball marks the gravitational height of the city's first piped water supply.

Across the street is a small iron fountain, a memorial known as Witches Well. This fountain marks the spot where, for about 250 years from the end of the 15th century, 300 so-called witches were burned at the stake.

Nearby is **Ramsay Garden,** built on the site of the house where Allan Ramsay the poet and writer lived. In 1736, he opened a theatre in the High Street which was promptly closed by magistrates, who believed that such light-hearted nonsense was inappropriate to the gravity of Scotland's capital.

Panoramic views of Edinburgh were provided by a 19th-century optician who installed a 'camera obscura' in the 17th-century **Outlook Tower** on Castle Hill. By using a lens and mirror, an image of the city is projected onto a saucer-shaped top.

Tolbooth Kirk is a 19th-century Gothic-style building which boasts the tallest spire in Edinburgh. It was built for the General Assembly of the Church of Scotland.

LEFT:
Ramsay Garden

ABOVE:
Outlook Tower on Castle Hill

St Giles' Cathedral stands on a site which has been used for worship since at least AD 845. The present Gothic style dates from 1829, though its main structure incorporates much older features – the pillars that support the 15th-century crown spire have been standing for 850 years. St Giles contains many monuments and memorials, including one to Robert Louis Stevenson and a stained-glass window dedicated to Robert Burns. An ornately carved Chapel of the Most Ancient and Most Noble Order of the Thistle, Scotland's highest order of chivalry, was added around 1910.

Although its proper title is the High Kirk of St Giles, it is known as St Giles' Cathedral and it has been at the centre of the nation's turbulent religious struggles. Scotland was Catholic until the Reformation in the 16th century, when John Knox became St Giles' minister. His zealous mission was to preach against Popery. Knox's statue, erected in 1706, stands against the cathedral wall at a spot where he is believed to have been buried.

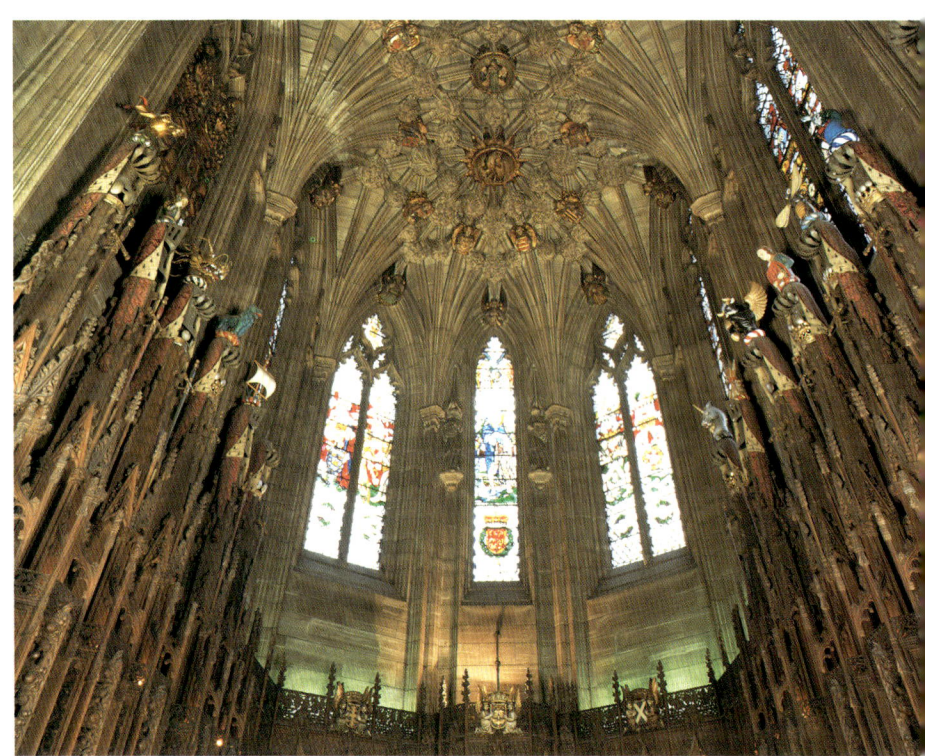

Lawnmarket, the second of the streets which form the Royal Mile, was originally the market place of the Old Town. Gladstone's Land is a largely 17th-century tenement, built by the merchant Thomas Gledstanes and restored by The National Trust for Scotland in the style of a typical house and shop of the period.

Behind it is Lady Stair's Close and the 17th-century house where Lady Stair, a fashionable society beauty, lived. It is now a museum containing mementoes of three great Scottish literary men – Robert Burns, Robert Louis Stevenson and Sir Walter Scott.

Edinburgh also spawned notorious villains. Deacon Brodie's Tavern is named after William Brodie, the inspiration for Stevenson's monster Dr Jekyll and Mr Hyde. Brodie was a town councillor by day and a burglar by night before he was caught and hanged in 1788.

Where Lawnmarket finishes, the **High Street** continues the Royal Mile. **Parliament Square** contains a statue of King Charles II on horseback. Parliament House was completed in 1639 for the Scottish Parliament but was only used for this purpose for about 70 years. It is now the home of Scotland's supreme courts and is noted for its 17th-century hammer-beam roof.

TOP LEFT:
Lady Stair's House

ABOVE:
St Giles' Cathedral with its crown-shaped spire

LEFT:
The Thistle Chapel, St Giles' Cathedral

RIGHT:
Mercat Cross

Near the west door of St Giles is the **Heart of Midlothian**, a heart made of granite blocks embedded in the road. It marks the site of the entrance to the Old Tolbooth city prison, built in 1446 and demolished in 1817. Superstitious citizens still spit on the heart to ward against being sent to prison.

Mercat Cross was the meeting place where merchants gathered to conduct their business. Royal proclamations were read out here, as important news still is today. The present structure, dating from the 19th century, incorporates parts of the original 14th-century Mercat Cross and was a gift from Prime Minister William Gladstone.

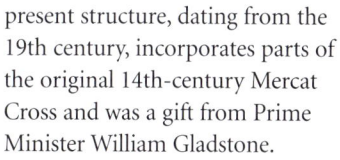

Tron Kirk, built in the 17th century and now a heritage centre, is named after a tron, or weighing machine, once situated on the site. Merchants were threatened that, if they were found guilty of cheating their customers, they would be punished by being nailed to the weighing beam by their ears!

Opposite St Giles is City Chambers, begun in 1753, where Edinburgh's Lord Provost and the City Council meet. The classically inspired building has, in its piazza, a statue of Alexander taming his horse Bucephalus to represent the power of the mind over brute force.

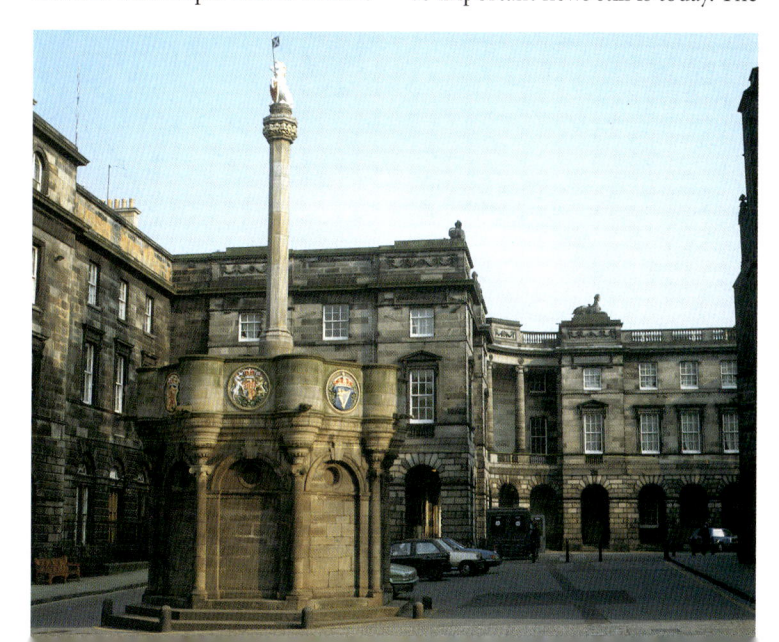

In the High Street stands **John Knox House** which dates from 1490. Knox is believed to have lived here between 1561 and 1572. On display in the Oak Room with its hand-painted ceiling are some of his artefacts.

On the same side of the street is Moubray House, which is even older. It has had many uses over the centuries, including tavern, home of Daniel Defoe and temperance hotel in the 18th century.

Canongate, the next section of the Royal Mile, contains one of Edinburgh's famous landmarks, the Tolbooth. It was built in the 16th century as a council chamber, court house and jail. Opposite is Huntly House, which was once a row of 16th-century houses and is now a museum of local history.

Canongate Kirk dates from the 17th century and was built originally to serve disgruntled and displaced worshippers when Charles II enlarged Holyrood Palace and converted the Abbey for the Knights of the Thistle.

White Horse Close is a picturesque courtyard once used in the 16th century as the Royal Mews. It was redeveloped as an inn and coaching stables and named after Queen Anne's white palfry.

LEFT:
John Knox House

BELOW LEFT:
The Tolbooth, Canongate

RIGHT:
Canongate Kirk

BELOW:
White Horse Close

IN 1688 KING JAMES VII
ORDAINED THAT THE MORTIFICATION
OF THOS. MOODIE GRANTED IN 1649 TO
BUILD A CHURCH SHOULD BE APPLIED
TO THE ERECTION OF THIS STRUCTURE

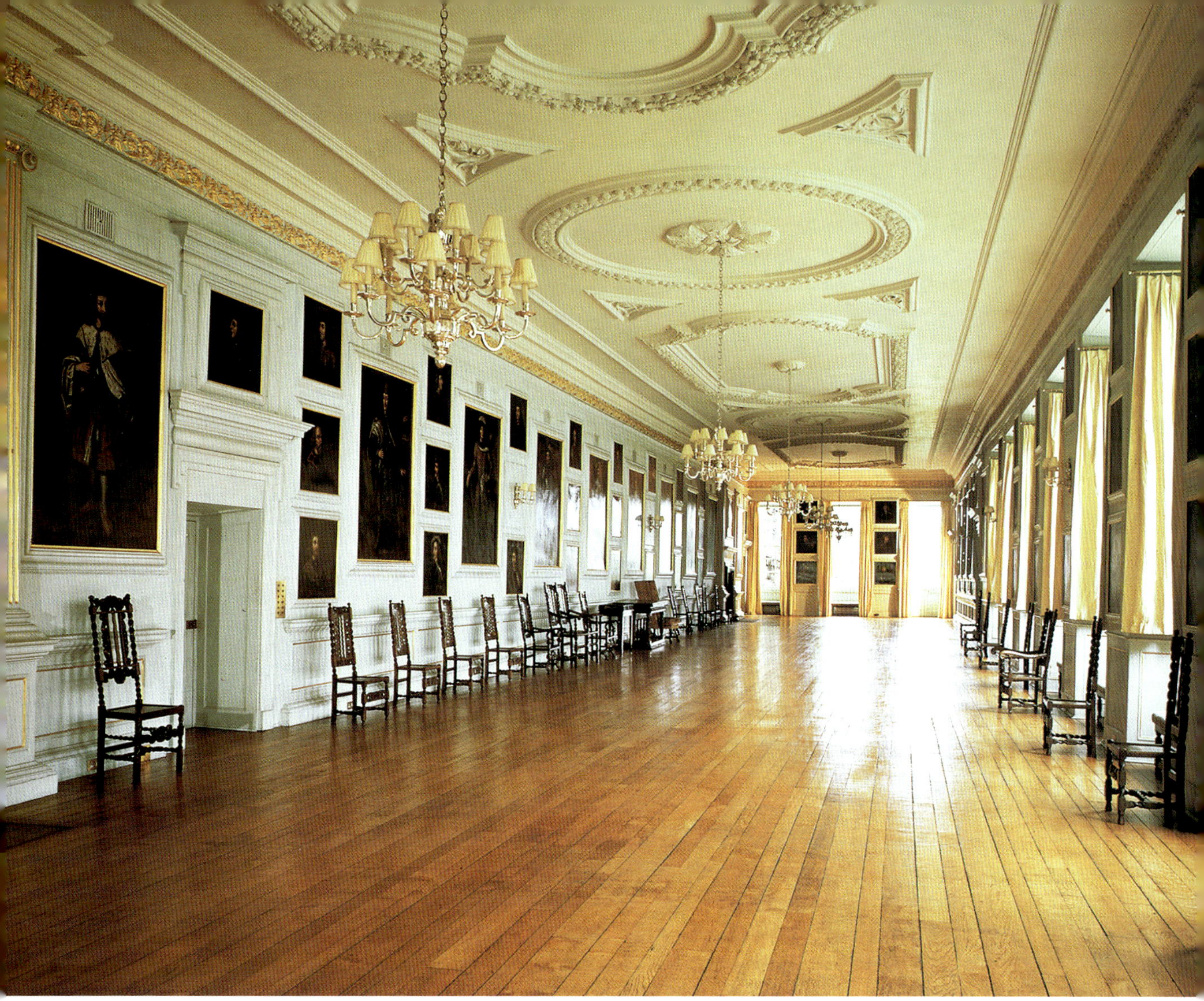

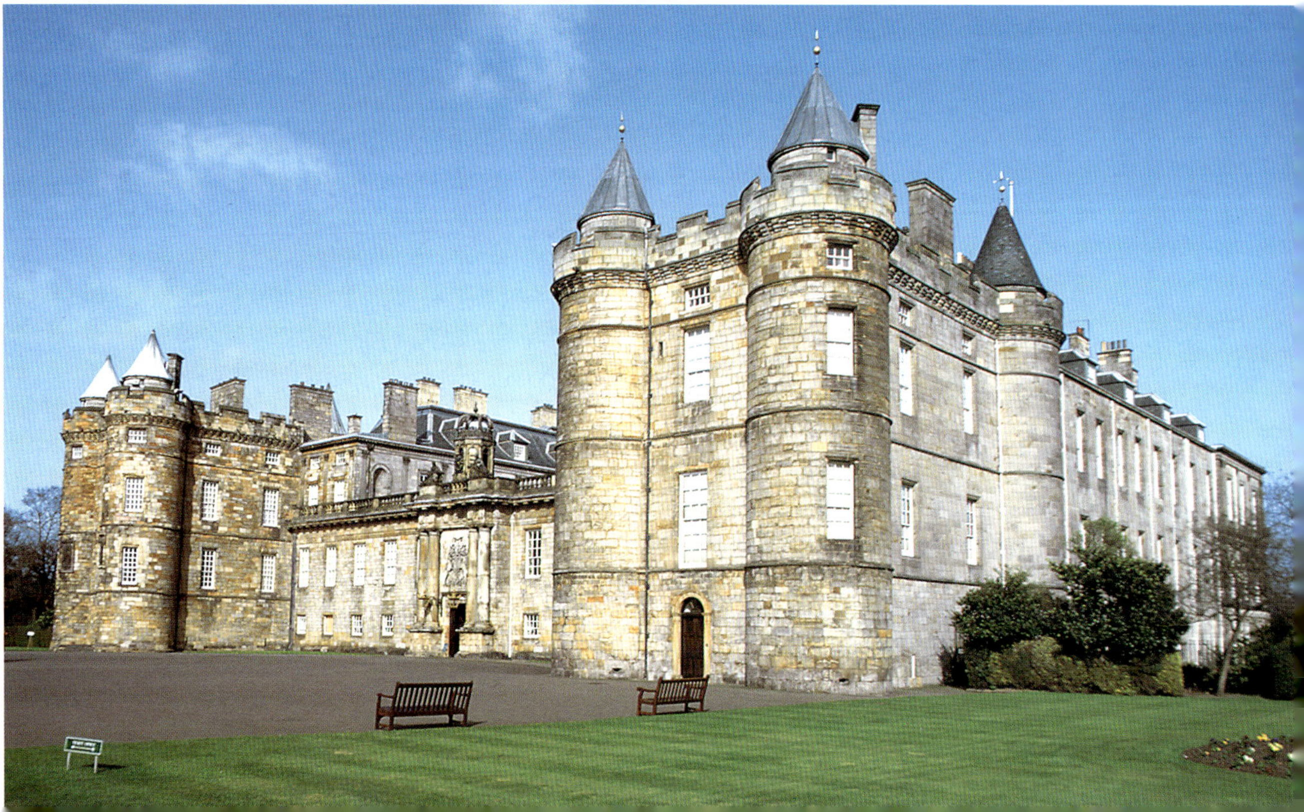

PALACE OF HOLYROOD

The **Palace of Holyrood** has been a part of Scotland's turbulent history for nearly nine centuries. Holyrood Abbey was initially founded in 1128 by David I. Subsequent Scottish monarchs found that they preferred to use the Abbey as a base rather than the Castle, and so the palace gradually developed. The **Abbey Church** itself fell into decline during the 18th century, and remains a ruin today.

Over the centuries though, improvements and refurbishments were carried out to the palace, perhaps the most noteworthy being the rebuilding in the 17th century by Charles II. He employed the skills of Sir William Bruce and the Duke of Lauderdale to enlarge the palace and make it more practical for royal usage. Today the **Palace of Holyrood** is the official royal residence in Scotland and is used extensively by the Queen for engagements and functions.

The palace treasures include some fine tapestries, 18th-century furniture, needlework panels sewn by Mary Queen of Scots, and the Darnley Jewel – a large locket of precious stones and enamel which dates from the 16th century. The **Great Gallery** contains portraits painted in the 17th century of over a hundred Scottish kings.

The Palace of Holyrood has witnessed some of the most poignant moments in Scottish history, particularly the tragic marriage of Mary Queen of Scots to Lord Darnley in 1565 and the murder of her secretary Rizzio in 1566. Bonnie Prince Charlie held court here during the Jacobite rebellion of 1745. In May 1999 the first Scottish Minister was appointed here, and the following month Queen Elizabeth II received the new members of the first Scottish Parliament since 1707.

ABOVE:
The Great Gallery in the Palace of Holyrood

LEFT:
Palace of Holyrood

RIGHT:
Holyrood Abbey

HOLYROOD PARK

The Palace of Holyrood stands at one corner of Holyrood Park. The park is dominated by **Arthur's Seat**, a long-dormant volcano, whose colossal bulk rises up 251 metres (823 feet) making it visible from many parts of the city. Visitors and residents alike are enticed to the summit for the spectacular views over the capital and the Firth of Forth. From the top, you can see not only the other two volcanoes of the Lothians, North Berwick Law and the Bass Rock, but, on a clear day, Ben Lomond as well!

In 1836 a small cave was discovered on Arthur's Seat containing a mysterious array of tiny coffins. There were 17 in all, and each measured no more than 10 centimetres (4 inches). Carved out of a solitary piece of wood, with decorations in tin on the sides and two brass pins to fix each lid, they had been arranged in three neat tiers. A perfectly formed, tiny figurine was discovered inside each one. The origin of these coffins remains a mystery, but some of them can be seen in the Royal Museum of Scotland in Queen Street.

Holyrood Park also houses the **Dynamic Earth** exhibition near Holyrood Palace. It gives a unique glimpse of 4,500 years of the Earth's history and is one of Edinburgh's most popular attractions.

On the south-eastern edge of Holyrood Park lies **Duddingston Loch**, home to an abundant variety of bird life. Grebe, sparrowhawk, kestrel, swan, heron, ducks and warblers all use this wildlife sanctuary just a short way from the city centre. It is popular not only with nature lovers, but, due to its idyllic setting, with walkers too.

ABOVE:
Salisbury Crags and Arthur's Seat

LEFT:
View of Duddingston Loch from Arthur's Seat

RIGHT:
The Dynamic Earth exhibition

OLD TOWN

The **Grassmarket**, at the foot of the Castle, was once one of the bloodiest sites of Edinburgh's Old Town. A small garden marks the place where hundreds of Covenanters – those who pledged themselves to defend Presbyterianism – and criminals died on the gallows, until public executions were stopped in 1784.

In this area lived Burke and Hare who carried out their grisly trade of supplying corpses for medical research. Nearby is West Bow, named because it was within an arrow's shot of the Castle. A passage at one corner of the Grassmarket leads to a section of the old City Wall, built after the Scots were slain by the English at the battle of Flodden Field in 1513. The wall forms a section of the boundary of George Heriot's School, founded by King James VI's goldsmith in the 17th century.

Another corner of the Grassmarket joins **Candlemaker Row**, named after the traditional craft of candlemaking. At the end of Candlemaker Row is Greyfriars Kirk, where the National Covenant was signed in 1638 by those who opposed Charles II's attempt to re-establish the Catholic faith.

ABOVE:
The Grassmarket below Edinburgh Castle

LEFT:
George Heriot's School

RIGHT:
Greyfriars Bobby

TOP RIGHT:
Candlemaker Row with the statue of Greyfriars Bobby

Edinburgh is the only city to have a dog on its list of citizens granted the freedom of the city – the statue of **Greyfriars Bobby** is at the top of Candlemaker Row. Following the death of his master, John Gray, in 1858, the young Skye terrier sustained a 14-year long vigil at his master's grave in Greyfriars Kirkyard.

Not much is known about John Gray. In her famous novel, *Greyfriars Bobby*, Eleanor Atkinson portrayed him as a shepherd from the Pentlands, but others claim that he was a policeman who trod the streets around the Grassmarket. The story of Bobby's outstanding faithfulness and loyalty, however, is undisputed.

The memorial, erected in his honour, has a statue of Bobby on a tall column above a twin level fountain. The two basins – one at waist height, the other at the kerb – were designed to symbolise the harmony between man and animal, allowing both to drink from the same source. The graves of both John Gray and Bobby can be found in the Kirkyard and a small bothy allows visitors to investigate the intriguing story further.

NEW TOWN

One man's vision led to the development of the **New Town**. George Drummond, the city's Lord Provost, suggested draining the Nor' Loch (now Princes Street Gardens) and in 1767 a 23-year old architect, James Craig, won a competition to design the area.

His plan – a simple and orderly pattern of squares, gardens and streets – symbolised the parliamentary union between England and Scotland in 1707. The focus was George Street, in honour of King George III, with Thistle Street and Rose Street (named after the national emblems of Scotland and England) on each side. George Street links Charlotte Square and St Andrew's Square, where the Royal Bank of Scotland and other financial institutions are based.

Charlotte Square was designed by Robert Adam in 1791. The Georgian House at number 7 has been restored to how it would have looked in the 18th century and is open to the public. Next door, Bute House is the official residence of the First Minister of the Scottish Parliament. These houses and those at numbers 26 to 31 are owned by The National Trust for Scotland.

The second phase of the development included the open spaces of Drummond Place and Royal Circus, the work of architect William Playfair. He was also responsible for several of the buildings on **Calton Hill**: the Parthenon-style National Monument, which was started in 1822 but never completed, the New Observatory, and a neo-classical memorial to the philosopher Dugald Stewart. The telescope-shaped Nelson's Monument was built to honour Admiral Lord Nelson. On top of the tower is a time ball which drops daily at one o'clock, the same time the cannon is fired at the Castle.

ABOVE:
Nelson Monument and the National Monument

FAR LEFT:
The Georgian House, Charlotte Square

LEFT:
Memorial to Dugald Stewart

RIGHT:
Princes Street with the Scott Monument

Princes Street, Edinburgh's main shopping street, is remarkable in having shops on one side only to give an unimpeded view of the Castle. **Scott Monument**, built in 1884 to commemorate Sir Walter Scott, is the tallest building in Princes Street and the largest memorial to a writer ever built.

The **National Gallery of Scotland**, a handsome classical building designed by William Playfair at the foot of the Mound, houses Old Masters and important works from almost every period in Western art.

Princes Street Gardens link the Old and New Towns.

19

AROUND EDINBURGH

Edinburgh's development beyond the Old and New Towns managed to retain some of the existing villages. **Dean Village** was a busy milling centre which, from the 12th century, used the Water of Leith to power the mills and granaries.

The Water of Leith also runs through the heart of the village of **Stockbridge**. Some of the village streets are named after the artist Henry Raeburn, who painted many powerful and wealthy figures of the 18th century and who developed the area. **The Royal Botanic Gardens** are close by.

The former Royal Yacht, *Britannia*, is moored at Leith on the banks of the Firth of Forth. The ship was launched on 16 April 1953. Much loved by Queen Elizabeth II and designed according to her wishes, *Britannia* made 968 official voyages and covered more than a million miles until she was decommissioned on 11 December 1997 and brought to Leith.

ABOVE:
The Forth Road Bridge from South Queensferry

FAR LEFT:
Britannia, the former Royal Yacht, at Leith

LEFT:
Dean Village

RIGHT:
Lauriston Castle

Lauriston Castle and gardens are on the northern edge of Edinburgh between Davidson Mains and Cramond. A fortified tower house was constructed here in 1590 by Sir Archibald Napier. During the 1820s the addition of a large extension transformed the castle into a Jacobean-style mansion.

Queensferry, 14 kilometres (9 miles) west of the city centre, grew up at an important crossing point, where the Firth of Forth is at its narrowest. The ferry crossing was named after Queen Margaret who landed nearby in 1067 on her way to Edinburgh Castle. Queensferry is the best vantage point to see the **Forth Bridges**. The rail bridge, built in 1890, was one of the greatest engineering feats of its time. The road suspension bridge was opened to traffic in 1964.

Nearby is **Hopetoun House**, Scotland's finest stately home. It dates from the 18th century and is set in beautiful parkland.

Only 5 kilometres (3 miles) from the city centre, **Craigmillar Castle** is one of the best-preserved medieval castles in Scotland. It stands on a rocky hilltop and offers superb views across the Lothians towards the Firth of Forth. Its strong connections with Mary Queen of Scots, who fled here after the murder of Rizzio, have ensured the castle remains one of Edinburgh's most important historic sites.

For centuries, residents and visitors to Edinburgh have made the short trip to **Portobello** to relax on the famous beach or walk the long promenade that runs all the way into **Musselburgh**. This bustling harbour, which has Arthur's Seat for a backdrop, is one of the most beautiful settings in the Forth Estuary. Musselburgh is steeped in history. In 1547 English forces defeated the superior Scottish army at the battle of Pinkie, while a short distance from the Pinkie Braes is Preston Grange Mining Museum. Mining was originally started by the monks of Newbattle Abbey and continued here for more than 800 years, until 1963.

ABOVE:
Craigmillar Castle

LEFT:
Musselburgh harbour with Arthur's Seat in the distance

RIGHT:
Traquair House

Crichton Castle, a few miles south of Dalkeith, close to Pathhead village, dates from 1400 and was built by John Crichton. In 1562 Mary Queen of Scots visited the castle for the marriage of Lord James Stewart to Lady Janet Hepburn. The well-preserved ruined castle is noted mainly for its oriel windows, corbel courses, turrets, arches, large corbels and vaulted rooms.

Traquair House, near Peebles to the south of Edinburgh, was one of the homes of the royal Stuart family. Dating back to the 10th century, it is said to be Scotland's oldest continuously inhabited house – William the Lion held court here in 1209. It contains relics of Mary Queen of Scots and a collection of Jacobite mementoes.

FESTIVITIES

The first **Edinburgh Festival** was held in 1947 and now attracts audiences from all over the world. For three weeks every year in August and September, several hundred artists give thousands of performances – of plays, revues, concerts, dance, mime, recitals and operas, not to mention film shows and art exhibitions, even displays of work on the pavements. The Festival includes the Military Tattoo on the Castle Esplanade.

In 1999, Edinburgh boasted the world's greatest **Hogmanay** party. The city continues to welcome in the new year with a tremendous fireworks display launched from the castle battlements. More than three tonnes of fireworks are released in just five minutes and can be seen from all over the city.

ABOVE: A Fringe theatre group performing at the Edinburgh Festival

TOP: Funfair during Hogmanay at the east end of Princes Street

24